# Year-Round Crafts for KIDS

Publications International, Ltd.

**Contributing Designers:** Lori Blankenship, Lisa Galvin,
Heidi King, and Sherri Osborn
**Contributing Illustrators:** Barbara Ball and Connie
Formby
**Icon Illustrators:** Terri and Joe Chicko

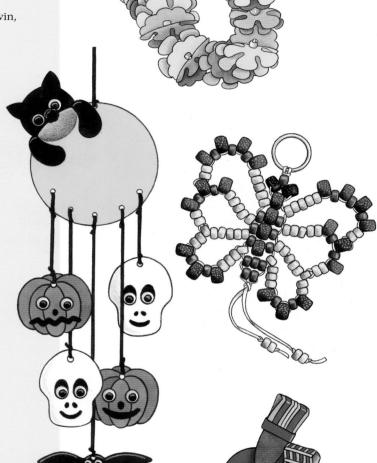

Louis Weber, CEO
Publications International, Ltd.
7373 North Cicero Avenue
Lincolnwood, Illinois 60712

Manufactured in China.

8 7 6 5 4 3 2 1

ISBN: 1-4127-1025-1

# Contents

## Fall

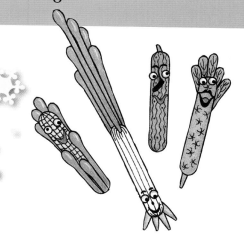

## Summer

## Winter

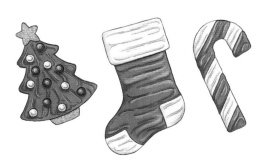

# Year-Round Crafts Mean Year-Round Fun!

## Dear Parents,

Just about everyone has made a Thanksgiving turkey out of their handprint or homemade Valentines for their family and friends. But there are so many other crafty ways to celebrate the holidays!

*Year-Round Crafts for Kids* offers tons of fun, interesting projects that are designed to keep your children busy the whole year long. From springtime flower bouquets and back-to-school projects to super summer flip-flops and way cool Christmas ornaments, kids can find crafts for all of their favorite holidays plus projects to commemorate the changing seasons. Best of all, some of the craft projects offer information about different cultures of the world and many may provide children with skills that could help them in school and everyday life.

Divided into four sections—Spring, Summer, Fall, and Winter—*Year-Round Crafts for Kids* includes simple crafts that require common craft materials, many of which you can probably find in your own home. Each project includes a list of materials needed to complete the craft as well as easy-to-follow instructions and step-by-step illustrations. Take the time to go over the instructions for each project carefully, and make sure you have all the materials on hand before you get started. Here are just a few of the basic craft materials that are required for most projects in this book:

- Paper: Since some of the book's projects include patterns that will need to be traced and cut out, be sure to have plenty of tracing paper on hand. When a craft project calls for scrap paper, recycle some of that computer paper and junk mail you have lying around the house!

- Glue: Most projects call for craft, or white, glue. This is a waterbase glue that can be thinned for easy application. Fabric glue, which is not water-soluble, holds up better outdoors or in projects that will be washed. You'll also need a glue gun for some of the projects. Be sure to use a low-temperature glue gun, and keep an eye on your child while he or she is using it.

- Paint: Waterbase acrylic paint is listed most frequently for the projects in this book. It is a vibrant form of paint that can be used on all surfaces. Acrylic paint dries permanently, but when wet it is easily cleaned up with water. Make sure your children clean painting tools thoroughly when they are finished painting.

- Chenille stems: Most chenille stems come in 12-inch lengths, so when a project calls for a chenille stem, that means a 12-inch stem.
- Art smock: Make sure your child wears a smock or one of your old shirts to protect clothes while working with paints and other messy materials such as clay.

Some children will be able to complete the crafts with little help, but there will be times when your assistance is needed. Other projects just need a watchful eye. So it's best if you and your child review the project together and then make a decision about your role.

Completing the projects in *Year-Round Crafts for Kids* should be an enjoyable, creative, energizing experience for your child. Encourage kids to create their own versions of projects, using their imagination as their guide. And don't forget to admire and praise the wonderful results!

## Hey, Kids!

The changing seasons can bring about so many fun things— the first day of school, the *last* day of school, the first winter snowfall, the first summer picnic at the park. Well, now you can celebrate these and so many other events and holidays with cool craft projects!

*Year-Round Crafts for Kids* is filled with ideas for arts and crafts projects, many of which would make great gifts for family and friends. Although we know you will want to get started on the cool projects right away, it is important to read these few basic steps before beginning any of the crafts.

- For any project or activity you decide to do, gather all your materials, remembering to ask permission first. If you need to purchase materials, take along this book, or make a shopping list so you know exactly what you need.
- Prepare your work area ahead of time, including covering any surface you work on with newspapers or an old, plastic tablecloth. Ask an adult if you're not sure whether to cover the kitchen table—but remember, it's better to be safe than sorry!
- Wear an apron or a smock when painting with acrylic paints; after the paint dries, it is permanent. If you do get paint on your clothes, wash them with soap and warm water immediately.

- Be sure an adult is nearby to offer help if you need it. And adult help is always needed if you will be using a glue gun, a craft knife, an oven, or anything else that may be dangerous.
- Be careful not to put any materials near your mouth. And make sure to watch out for small items, such as beads, around little kids and pets.

- Be sure to use a low-temperature glue gun. Do not touch the nozzle or the freshly applied glue; it may still be hot. And be sure to use the glue gun with adult permission only!
- Clean up afterward, and put away all materials and tools. Leaving a mess one time may mean you hear the word "no" the next time you ask to make something!
- Have fun, and be creative!

## Pattern Perfect

Many of the projects featured in this book include patterns to help you complete the craft more easily. When a project's instructions tell you to cut out a shape according to the pattern, trace the pattern from the book onto tracing paper, using a pencil. If the pattern has an arrow with the word *FOLD* next to a line, it is a half pattern. Fold a sheet of tracing paper in half, and open up the paper. Place the fold line of the tracing paper exactly on top of the fold line of the pattern, and trace the pattern with a pencil. Then refold and cut along the line, going through both layers. Open the paper for the full pattern.

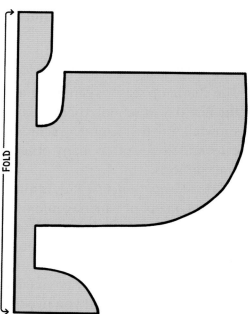

## Ready, Set, Go!

All of the projects presented in this book, from the simplest bookmark to the most elaborate beaded key chain, are just ideas to get you started crafting. Feel free to play around with the designs by changing the colors, choosing different materials, or embellishing in any number of unique ways. Once you are comfortable with these crafts, let your imagination really go wild and dream up some original crafts using these merely as a jumping-off point. There's no limit to what you can create!

# Springtime Fun Finger Puppets

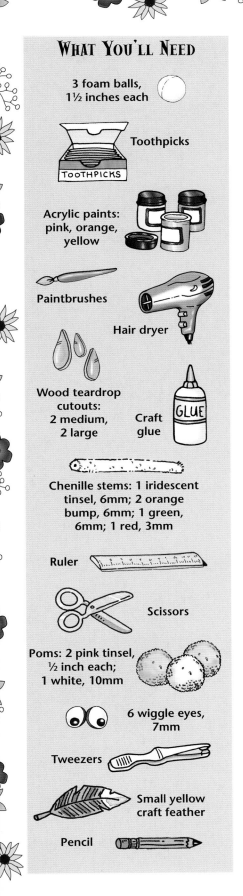

## What You'll Need

3 foam balls, 1½ inches each

Toothpicks

Acrylic paints: pink, orange, yellow

Paintbrushes

Hair dryer

Wood teardrop cutouts: 2 medium, 2 large

Craft glue

Chenille stems: 1 iridescent tinsel, 6mm; 2 orange bump, 6mm; 1 green, 6mm; 1 red, 3mm

Ruler

Scissors

Poms: 2 pink tinsel, ½ inch each; 1 white, 10mm

6 wiggle eyes, 7mm

Tweezers

Small yellow craft feather

Pencil

**1** Insert a toothpick into each foam ball to help you handle the balls while you decorate them. Paint each ball a different color. Dry the balls with a hair dryer set on a warm temperature, turning them around to dry all sides. Paint 2 medium wood teardrops orange for the duckbill and 2 large teardrops pink for the bunny ears. Dry the wood cutouts with a hair dryer.

Spring  7

**2** To make the bunny ears, put a drop of glue onto the pointed end of a pink teardrop shape and push the end into the top of the pink ball. Repeat for the other ear. Cut two 2½-inch lengths from the iridescent tinsel chenille stem. Fold one length in half and insert it into the ball just in front of an ear. Repeat with the other chenille stem piece for the other ear. For the bunny's cheeks, glue the pink tinsel poms side by side toward the bottom of the pink foam ball. Glue the white pom just above the cheeks for the nose. Use tweezers to help you glue on 2 wiggle eyes.

**3** To make the duck finger puppet, pinch the top of the yellow foam ball between your thumb and index finger to make an egg shape. For the duckbill, apply glue to the pointed ends of the orange teardrop shapes and insert them into the ball, one on top of the other, toward the bottom of the duck's head. Insert the small yellow feather into the top of the head, and glue on 2 wiggle eyes.

**4** For the flower finger puppet, cut the orange chenille stems apart between bumps. Bend each bump into a flower petal. Add a drop of glue to the ends of 1 petal and insert it into the side of the orange foam ball. Repeat with the remaining petals, working around the foam ball. Cut the green chenille stem in half, then fold each length to create 2 leaves. Put glue on the ends of the leaves and insert them into the ball behind the petals. Glue on 2 wiggle eyes. Cut 2 inches from the red chenille stem, and bend the piece into a smile. Attach the smile to the flower face with glue.

**5** Use the sharpened end of the pencil to create a finger hole at the bottom of each finger puppet, gradually turning the pencil to make the hole large enough for your finger to fit into.

8 ❀ **Spring**

# Petal Posies

## What You'll Need

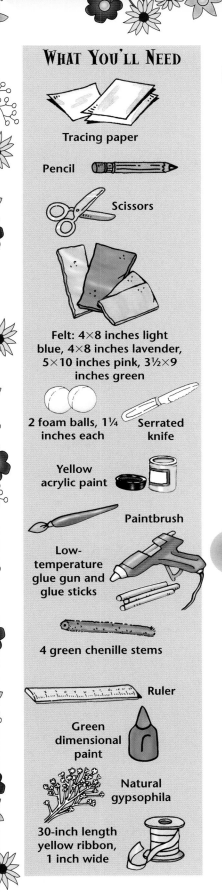

Tracing paper

Pencil

Scissors

Felt: 4×8 inches light blue, 4×8 inches lavender, 5×10 inches pink, 3½×9 inches green

2 foam balls, 1¼ inches each

Serrated knife

Yellow acrylic paint

Paintbrush

Low-temperature glue gun and glue sticks

4 green chenille stems

Ruler

Green dimensional paint

Natural gypsophila

30-inch length yellow ribbon, 1 inch wide

**1** Use the patterns on page 11 to trace and cut out the following: 2 round flowers from light blue felt, 2 round flowers from lavender felt, 2 pointed flowers from pink felt, and 6 leaves from green felt. Have an adult help you cut the foam balls in half with the serrated knife. Paint 3 foam ball halves with yellow paint; discard the remaining ball half. Let paint dry, then apply another coat. Glue the flat side of a ball half to the center of 1 blue flower. To give the flower a dimensional look, apply a line of glue around the very bottom edge of the foam ball and bend up the petals around the ball. Hold until set (be careful, glue can be hot!). Repeat for 1 pink flower and 1 lavender flower; set aside the other flowers.

**2** To make a flower stem, glue 1 inch of one end of a green chenille stem to the back of the blue felt flower. Align the edges of the flower with the other blue felt flower piece, sandwiching the chenille stem between them. Apply a line of glue between the layers near the edge, then press the edges together. Repeat for the pink and lavender flowers.

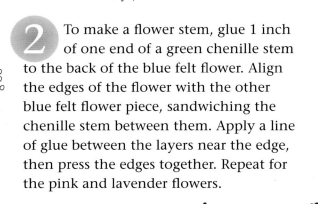

**3** Add veins on the leaves with green dimensional paint; let dry. Glue 5 leaves to 3 flower stems; set aside the remaining leaf.

**4** Add sprigs of gypsophila among the flowers. Make a bow out of the matching ribbon. Wrap the remaining chenille stem around the middle of the bow, then wrap the chenille stem around all the flower stems. Twist the chenille stem ends together in the back, then trim and fold over the ends. Glue the remaining leaf to the back of the uppermost flower.

# Patterns

# Lucky Sprouts

## WHAT YOU'LL NEED

Compressed sponge

Pencil

Scissors

Plate or pie pan

Quick-sprout seeds, such as cress or alfalfa

Plastic wrap

Markers (optional)

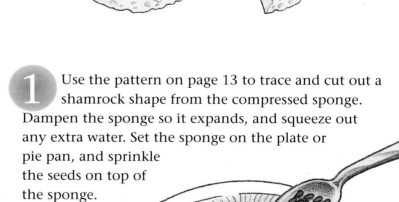

**1** Use the pattern on page 13 to trace and cut out a shamrock shape from the compressed sponge. Dampen the sponge so it expands, and squeeze out any extra water. Set the sponge on the plate or pie pan, and sprinkle the seeds on top of the sponge.

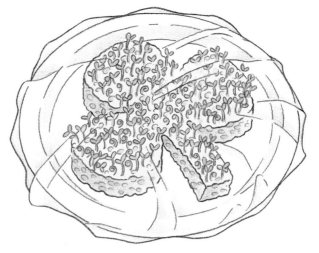

**2** Your seeds should sprout in a few days (see instructions on the seed package) if you take good care of them! During the night, cover the sponge lightly with plastic wrap to help it stay moist. During the day, place your sponge in a sunny spot, making sure the sponge stays wet (water around the sponge; do not put water directly on the seeds).

**3** For variety, draw and cut out different shapes from the compressed sponge. You can even try sprinkling seeds over just certain areas of the sponge. For example, you could cut out a shape that looks like a person's head and draw on a face with markers. Then sprinkle the seeds over the area where hair would grow. Pretend he's a leprechaun for even more luck!

## Pattern

### Did You Know?
The first St. Patrick's Day parade took place not in Ireland but in New York City on March 17, 1762.

# May Day Colorful Lei

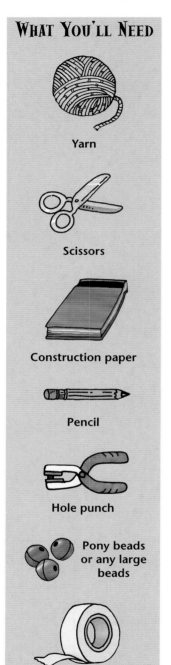

1 Cut a length of yarn to hang loosely around your neck (make sure you cut it a little longer than you want it so you have room to tie the ends of the yarn together).

Use the patterns on page 15 to trace and cut colorful flower shapes out of construction paper. (If you want flowers that will stand up to a little more wear and tear, make them out of craft foam; use tissue paper for more delicate flowers.) Punch a hole in the center of each flower.

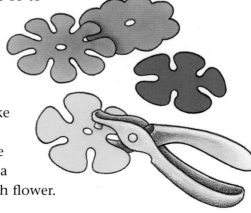

**2** Tie a knot at one end of the piece of yarn. String 6 to 10 beads onto the yarn (this will be the part of the lei that touches the back of your neck). Then alternate flowers and beads however you want. If you have a hard time stringing the beads onto the yarn, wrap a small piece of tape around the end of the yarn to stiffen it.

**3** Once you get the design you want and the yarn is almost full of flowers and beads, end just as you started, with 6 to 10 beads. Tie the end in a knot. Then tie the two ends of the yarn together, and wear your lei with pride!

### Did You Know?
May Day is celebrated as a festival marking the reappearance of flowers during the spring. People in Hawaii celebrate May Day by giving flower leis to each other.

## Patterns

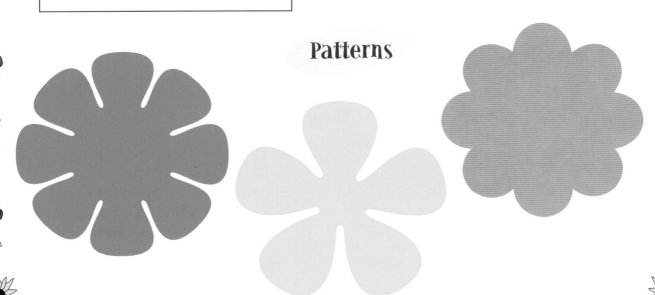

# Maraca Mania

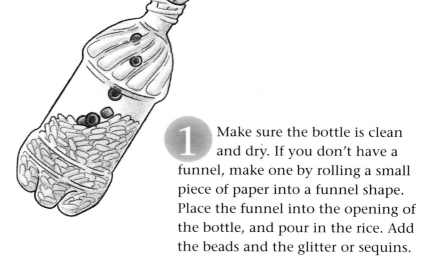

## What You'll Need

Clean, empty 16-ounce plastic bottle with cap

Funnel or paper

⅓ cup rice

Rice

Beads: ⅓ cup each red, green, white

Glitter or sequins: few teaspoons each red, green, white

GLUE

Glue

Ribbon: red, green, white

Scissors

Fabric Paint

Fabric paint: red, green, white

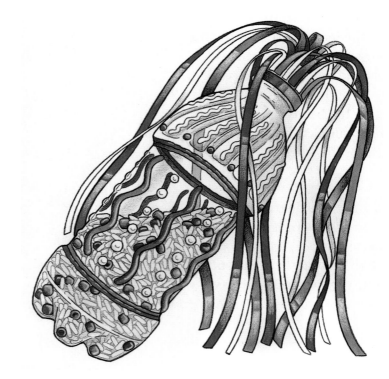

**1** Make sure the bottle is clean and dry. If you don't have a funnel, make one by rolling a small piece of paper into a funnel shape. Place the funnel into the opening of the bottle, and pour in the rice. Add the beads and the glitter or sequins.

2 Once you have enough rice, beads, and glitter or sequins in the bottle, spread glue along the edge of the bottle top. Replace the cap, and let the glue dry.

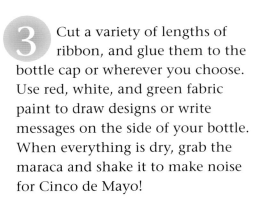

3 Cut a variety of lengths of ribbon, and glue them to the bottle cap or wherever you choose. Use red, white, and green fabric paint to draw designs or write messages on the side of your bottle. When everything is dry, grab the maraca and shake it to make noise for Cinco de Mayo!

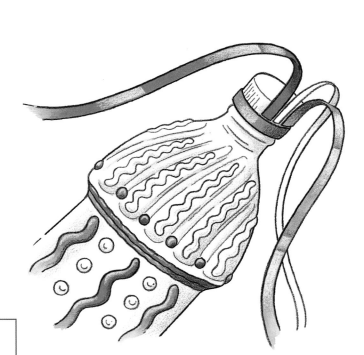

## Did You Know?

Cinco de Mayo, which means "Fifth of May" in Spanish, is a holiday to celebrate the Mexican army's victory over the French at the Battle of Puebla on May 5, 1862.

## WHAT YOU'LL NEED

12×18 inches blue craft foam

Ruler

Pencil

Scissors

Tracing paper

⅛-inch hole punch

5 feet blue plastic lacing

32 matching pony beads

9×6 inches multicolor adhesive craft foam

Adhesive-back hook-and-loop dots

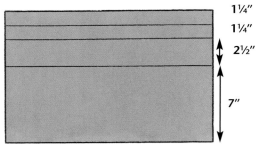

1¼"
1¼"
2½"
7"

**1** Along the shorter edge of the blue foam, measure and mark 2 strips 1¼ inches wide (for the strap) and 1 strip 2½ inches wide. Cut out the strips. Using the pattern on page 20, trace and cut out 2 side panels from the 2½-inch-wide strip (copy the pattern markings). The remaining foam piece should measure about 7 inches wide. This will be for the pouch. Round the corners of the pouch piece on one side.

**2** Starting ¼ inch from the squared edge of the pouch piece, measure and mark 26 points ½ inch apart and ¼ inch in from the side edge. Repeat on the other side. Punch holes at all points on all the pieces, including the side panels.

**3** Cut a 36-inch length of plastic lacing. Line up the square edge of one side panel with one edge of the pouch piece. Thread the lacing through the first holes of each section, and leave a 10-inch tail on the side panel side. Continue lacing through the matching holes, using a basic sewing stitch, until all the holes are used. Be sure to keep the edges even and leave a 10-inch tail. Repeat on the other side.

**4** Thread each tail through the top 2 holes on the side panel (the lace ends should end up on the outside of the side panel). Position one end of a strap piece over the holes at the top of a side panel. Use a pencil to mark points through the punched holes of the side panel to help you punch holes on the strap. Thread one lace end through the top hole on the strap, then thread the same lace diagonally to the bottom hole on the strap. Repeat with the other lace end (lace should have formed an *X*). Thread the lace ends through the opposite bottom strap holes. Tie the ends in a knot. Thread 3 pony beads on the remaining lacing, and tie a double knot on each end to hold the beads in place. Trim excess lacing. Repeat on the other side.

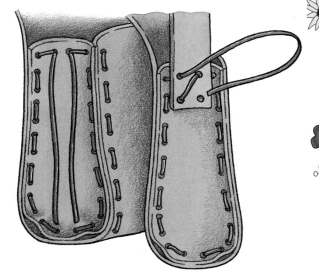

**5** Overlap the straps to desired length to fit over your shoulder. Holding the strap pieces in place, punch 4 holes in a square about ½ inch apart and about ¼ inch from the edges of the straps. Cut a 12-inch length of lacing, then thread the lacing down through one bottom hole and up through the other bottom hole. Bring the ends together evenly, cross the lace ends to form an *X*, then thread them down through the top holes. Lace each end back up through the bottom holes, then tie a knot to hold in place. Thread 2 pony beads on each end of the lacing, and tie a double knot on each end to hold the beads in place. Trim excess lacing. Repeat on the other overlapped section of the strap.

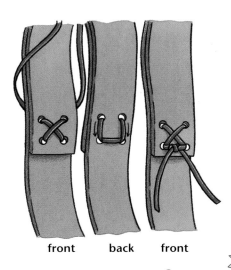

front        back        front

**6** Trace and cut out 3 flowers from the multicolor craft foam using the pattern on this page. Copy all markings, and punch holes at the points. Using 4 inches of lacing for each flower, thread the length of lacing through the holes, then tie a knot. Thread 2 pony beads on each end of the lacing, and tie a double knot at each end to hold the beads in place. Remove paper backing and stick the flowers to desired locations on the purse. Remove the paper backing from the loop dots and place them under the purse flap. Press the hook dots on the loop dots, then remove the backing from the hook dots and attach them to the front of the purse.

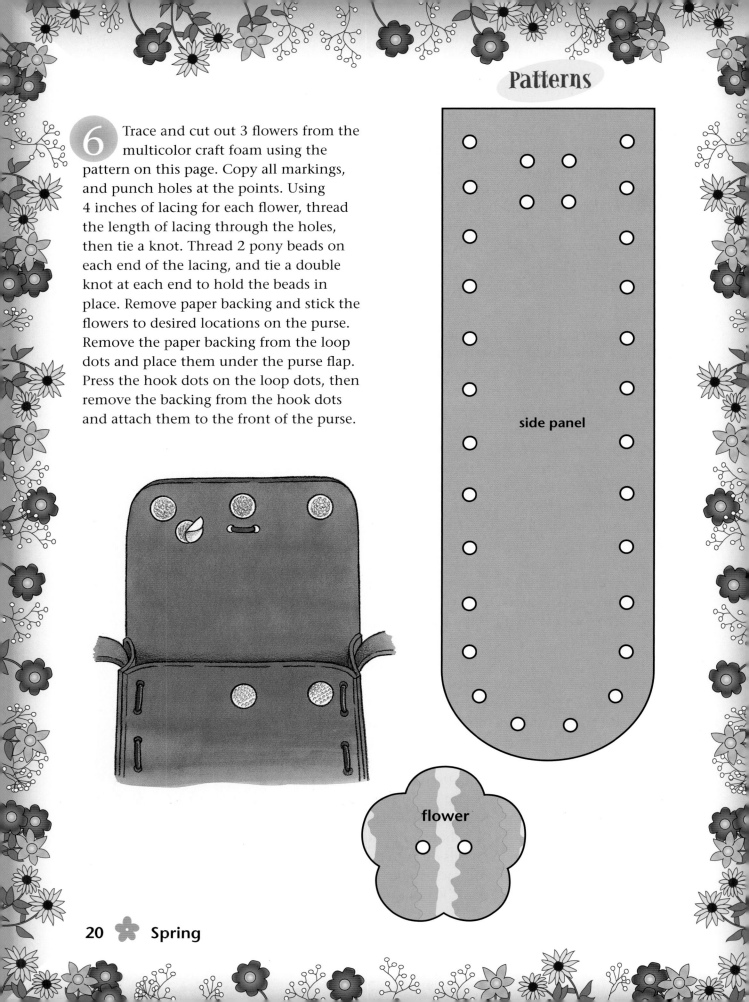

side panel

flower

# Cool Camp Frame

## What You'll Need

6½×7¼-inch wood frame

Sandpaper

Soft cloth     Acrylic paint

Paintbrushes

Wood craft picks

Scissors     Craft glue

Fine-point permanent markers     Wood craft spoon

Ruler

 Waterbase varnish, satin finish

 10-inch length ribbon, ¹⁄₁₆ inch (girl only)

Camp photo

**1** Ask an adult to help you take apart the wood frame, and set aside the frame backing and glass. Use sandpaper to remove any rough edges on the wood frame. Wipe the frame with a soft cloth to remove dust, then paint the frame in desired color with a paintbrush. Let dry 2 hours.

**2** Arrange 13 craft picks on a flat surface for the camp sign, alternating the direction of the picks as shown. Lay 2 craft picks across the sign vertically, and cut off any excess wood. Glue the 2 picks to the sign; let dry 2 hours. Paint the sign desired color. Let dry 1 hour, then use permanent markers to write your name, "Camp is Fun," or anything else you want.

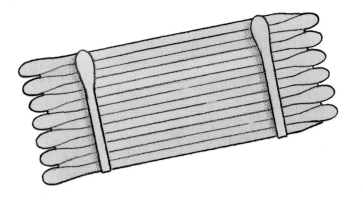

**3** To make the head of the boy or girl, measure and cut 1½ inches from the smallest end of the craft spoon. Sand any rough edges. Refer to the illustration to cut craft picks for the hair, ears, and fingers. Paint the head, fingers (if you're making a boy), ears, and hair desired colors. Let dry 1 hour. Glue the hair and ears onto the head to make a boy or girl. Use the the markers to add a face.

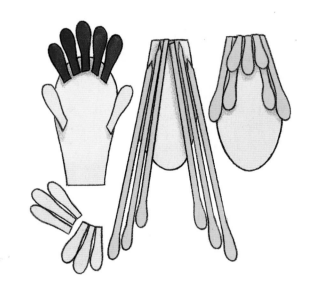

**4** Glue the head (and fingers for a boy) to the sign, then glue the sign to the top of the frame. Let dry 2 hours. Paint all the wood with the waterbase varnish. Let dry 1 hour or as directed by the manufacturer. If you're making a girl, tie the ribbon in a bow and glue it to the top of the head. Have an adult help you put the frame back together. Be sure to insert a camp photo in the frame to show how much fun you had this summer!

# Wingin' It

## WHAT YOU'LL NEED

6-foot length clear plastic lanyard

24mm split ring

Beads: 26 royal blue baby pony, 2 black glitter pony, 14 purple glitter pony, 34 light blue baby pony, 22 lavender baby pony, 10 blue glitter pony

Nail clippers

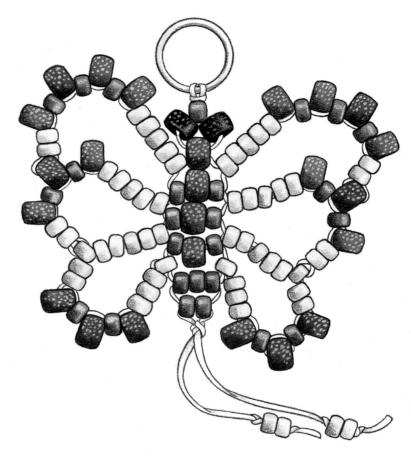

**1** Fold the lanyard in half, and slip the looped end through the split ring. Pull the cut ends up through the loop and pull tight. String a royal blue baby pony bead onto the left strand and slide it all the way up. Weave the right strand through the bead from right to left. String 1 black glitter pony bead onto each strand for the eyes, then add a purple glitter pony bead to the left strand. Weave the right strand through the purple glitter bead from right to left. Be sure to keep the lanyard flat as you weave it from one row to the next.

**2** To make the first "sidepath" of the right butterfly wing, string beads 1–15 on the right strand. Leave a little space between the beads, and weave back through, skipping the larger beads (beads 12, 10, 8, and 6). Pull tightly as you weave back, allowing the beads to curve as shown. Repeat to make the first sidepath of the left butterfly wing with the left strand. Add 1 royal blue baby pony, 1 purple glitter pony, and 1 royal blue baby pony to the left strand. Weave the right strand through the same 3 beads right to left.

**3** String the second sidepath on each side of the butterfly. As you weave back toward the body, make sure to skip bead 15 from the first sidepath. Similarly, after stringing the third sidepath, skip bead 12 from the middle sidepath as you weave back toward the body.

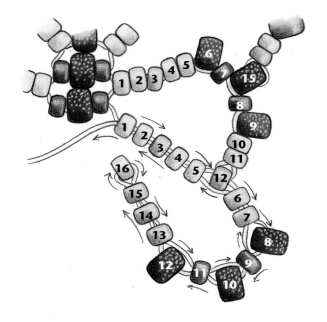

**4** Lace the last bead (16) of both lower wings to the body as a bead between rows. Use the bead diagram on page 24 to finish the last 2 rows.

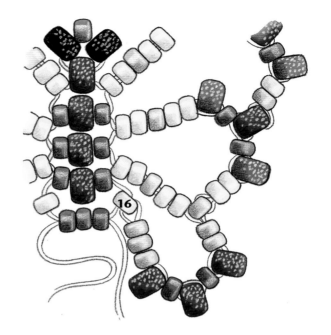

**5** Tie the lanyard ends together in an overhand knot. To do this, twist both lanyard ends into a loop and then pull the free ends through the loop. Tie a double knot toward the end of each strand. Thread a lavender bead and a light blue bead on each end, then tie a double knot on each strand to hold the beads in place (see illustration on page 23). Trim excess lanyard with nail clippers, leaving ¼-inch ends.

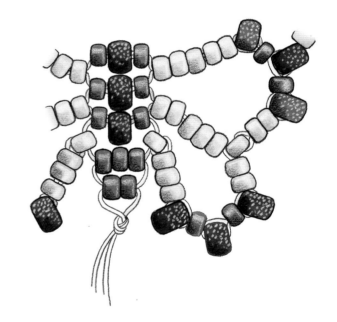

## Try This!

Once you have the basic beading techniques down, use different color beads to create all kinds of butterflies. Try making a monarch with orange, black, and white beads.

# Festive Fireworks T-Shirt

## WHAT YOU'LL NEED

Clean, white T-shirt

Cardboard

Scissors

2 spray bottles

Water

1 cup
1/2 cup
1/4 cup

Measuring cup

Red and blue fabric paint, 1 ounce each

Fabric Paint

Paintbrush

 **1** Be sure to cover yourself and your work area—this is a very messy project! You may even want to work outside. Cut a piece of cardboard so it fits inside the T-shirt, and slide it inside the shirt. This will prevent the paint from soaking through from one side of the shirt to the other. Lay the shirt flat on your work surface.

**2** Add about ⅓ cup of water to each spray bottle. Empty most of the red fabric paint into a spray bottle. Empty most of the blue paint into the other spray bottle. You need to thin the paint just enough so it can be squirted out of the bottle, so you may need to add more water than this (add just a small amount of water at a time).

**3** Now for the really fun part! Squirt red and blue starburst designs onto the shirt until it looks the way you want it. Wait for one side of the shirt to dry (about 1 hour), then flip the shirt over and paint the other side. Let dry.

**4** Use a paintbrush and the remaining fabric paint you did not put into the spray bottles to highlight different areas of your design. Let dry. Wear your shirt on the Fourth of July—or any day—with pride! (To care for your shirt, wash it in cold water and hang it up or lay it flat to dry.)

# On-the-Go Lap Desk

**Adult help needed**

## WHAT YOU'LL NEED

9×12-inch chalkboard

Pencil

Red acrylic paint

Small paintbrush

White paint pen

2-inch-deep plastic container, less than 9×12 inches

Low-temperature glue gun and glue sticks

**1** Trace and cut out the pattern on page 29, then trace the star shape on the front of the chalkboard as many times as you want to create a nice design.

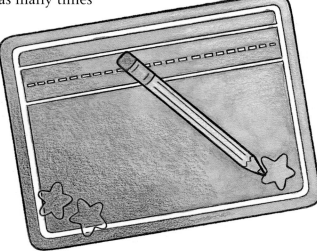

**2** Paint the star shapes with the red paint. Let dry, then apply another coat of paint. Add small white detail lines around each star with the paint pen.

**3** Center the chalkboard over the top of the container, then glue in place. Let dry. Fill your lap desk with everything you need for a summer road trip!

### Try This!
Instead of a plastic container, you could glue your decorated chalkboard on top of a pillow or a fabric pouch filled with small beans or foam pellets.

**Pattern**

# Funtime Flip-Flops

**Adult help needed**

## What You'll Need

Foam flip-flops

2-yard length grosgrain or woven ribbon, 2 inches wide

Scissors

Low-temperature glue gun and glue sticks

2 plastic or silk flowers (about 1 to 2 inches diameter) or 2 small plastic frogs

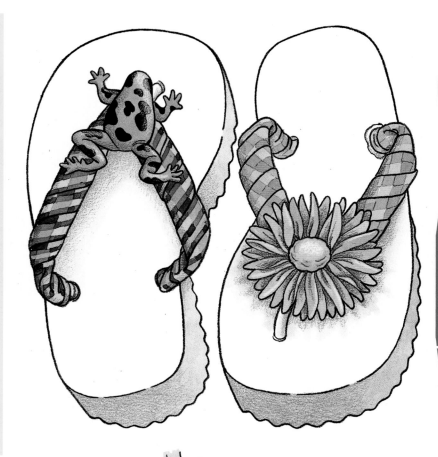

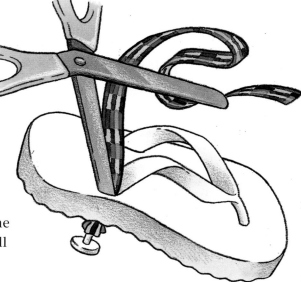

**1** Cut the ribbon into two equal lengths. Loosen one side of a flip-flop thong by pushing it down through the bottom of the shoe. Ask an adult to help you use the tip of the scissors to poke the end of one length of ribbon through the hole on one side. Pull the ribbon so about 1 inch hangs underneath the flip-flop. Using the glue gun, fill the hole with glue, then pull the thong up so it fits back into the hole on the bottom. Make sure the end of the ribbon is still visible from the bottom of the shoe.

**2** Working on the top of the flip-flop, wrap the ribbon around the thong so the plastic is completely covered. Overlap the edges each time you wrap the ribbon around to make sure it's secure. When you reach the other side of the thong, secure the end of the ribbon through the hole in the bottom of the flip-flop as you did in step 1.

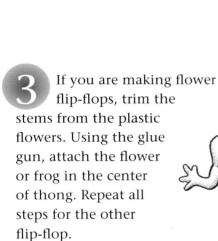

**3** If you are making flower flip-flops, trim the stems from the plastic flowers. Using the glue gun, attach the flower or frog in the center of thong. Repeat all steps for the other flip-flop.

## Try This!
Don't stop with frogs or flowers! You can make all kinds of fun flip-flops using plastic bugs, cute erasers, or whatever else you dream up!

# Totally Buggy Clips

## What You'll Need

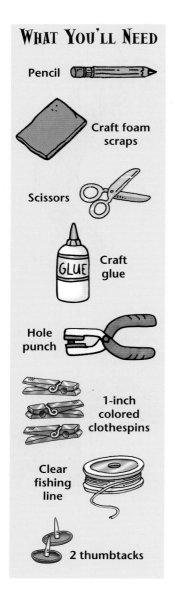

- Pencil
- Craft foam scraps
- Scissors
- Craft glue
- Hole punch
- 1-inch colored clothespins
- Clear fishing line
- 2 thumbtacks

**1** Use the patterns on page 34 to trace and cut bug shapes out of various colors of craft foam.

**2** To make a ladybug, glue 2 ladybug wings on top of a ladybug body, keeping the wings slightly apart in the middle. Use the hole punch to make small circles out of craft foam; glue them to the top of the ladybug wings. For the butterfly and dragonfly, glue a body cutout to a wing cutout. Let dry.

**3** Turn the bugs over, and glue a clothespin to the back of each bug. Let dry. String the fishing line along a wall, and secure it with a thumbtack on each end. Clip your buggy clothespins onto the line to hang your very best photos and artwork!

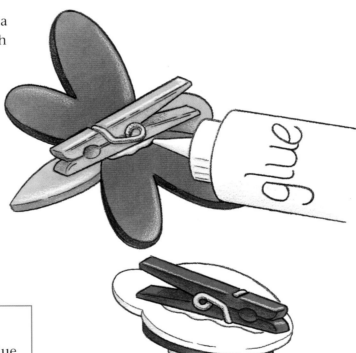

## Try This!

Instead of mini clothespins, glue the buggy foam shapes onto adhesive-back magnet strips. Then use them to display your best artwork or top-notch tests on the refrigerator for all to see!

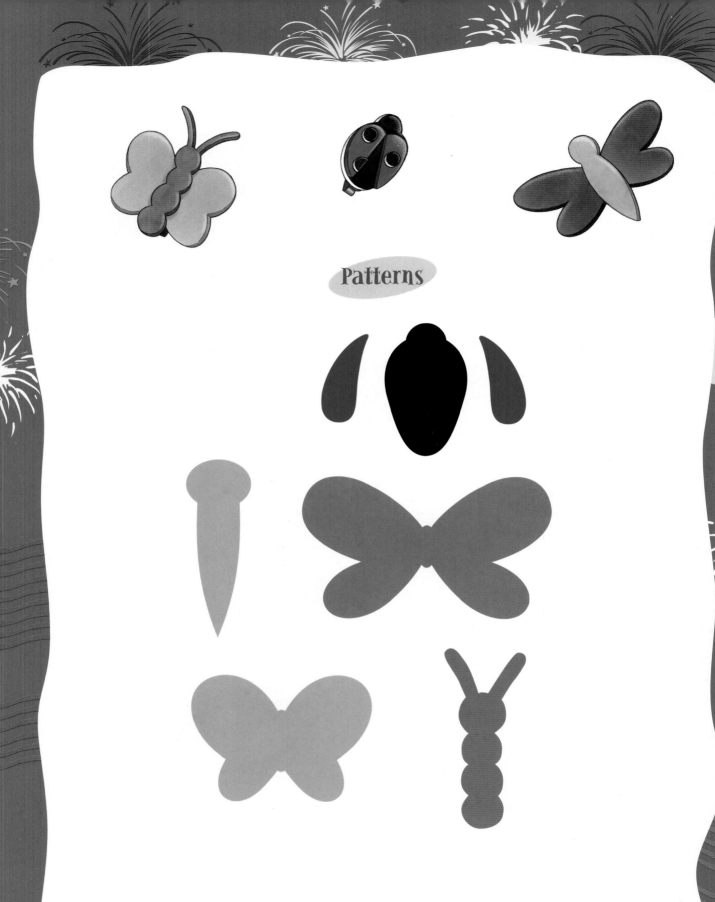

Patterns

# Veggie Magnets

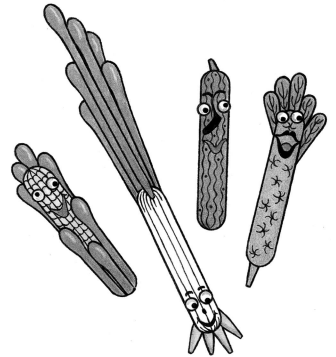

10×10 inches adhesive-back shelf paper

Tape

20 wood craft picks, 3½ inches long each

Ruler

Pencil

Scissors

Acrylic paint: brown, orange, green, yellow, white

Paintbrushes

4 mini wood craft sticks, ⅜×2½ inches each

Fine-point permanent markers: black, red

8 wiggle eyes, 5mm

Tweezers

Craft glue

½×2½-inch strip adhesive-back magnet

**1** Remove the backing from the shelf paper and place it on a flat surface with the adhesive side up. Use tape to hold down the corners. Measure and mark ½ inch from the pointed ends of 5 craft picks. Cut each pick at the marking. Place the pointed pieces on the shelf paper to hold while painting. Paint 4 pointed pieces brown for the onion roots and 1 piece orange for the tip of the carrot. Lay all the remaining craft picks and sticks on the shelf paper, leaving a little space between each piece. Paint the remaining craft picks green. Refer to the illustration to paint the mini craft sticks for each vegetable. Let dry 1 hour, then turn over and paint the back sides. Let dry 1 hour.

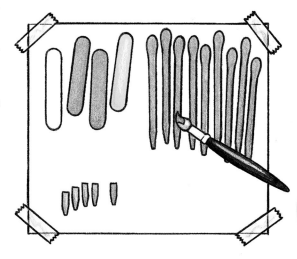

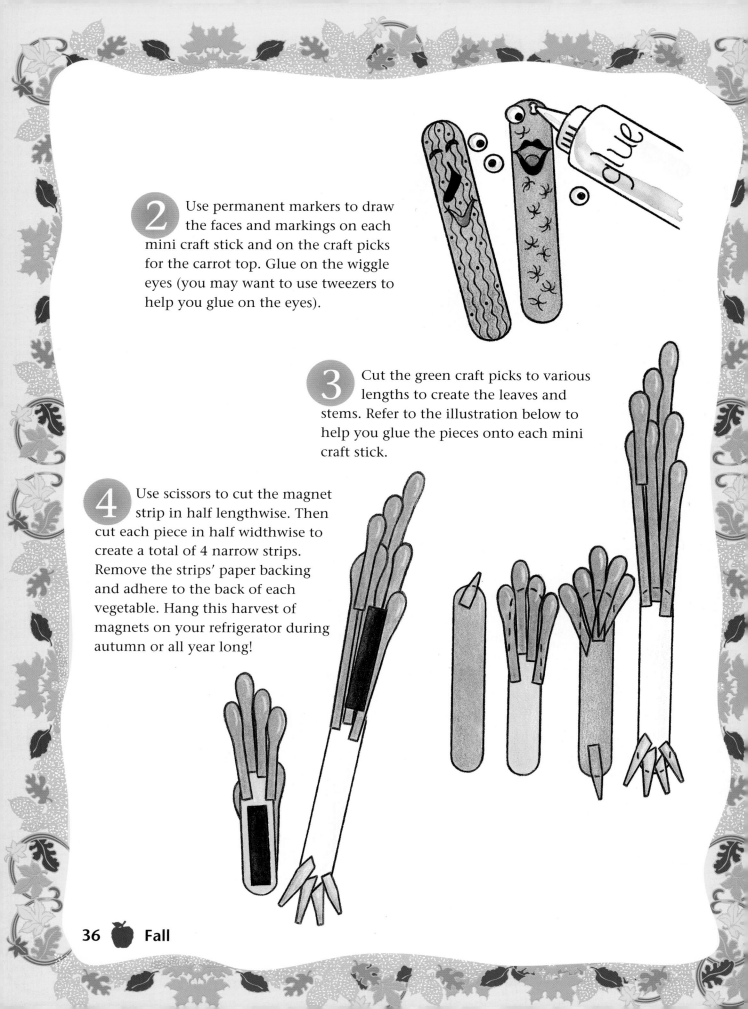

**2** Use permanent markers to draw the faces and markings on each mini craft stick and on the craft picks for the carrot top. Glue on the wiggle eyes (you may want to use tweezers to help you glue on the eyes).

**3** Cut the green craft picks to various lengths to create the leaves and stems. Refer to the illustration below to help you glue the pieces onto each mini craft stick.

**4** Use scissors to cut the magnet strip in half lengthwise. Then cut each piece in half widthwise to create a total of 4 narrow strips. Remove the strips' paper backing and adhere to the back of each vegetable. Hang this harvest of magnets on your refrigerator during autumn or all year long!

# Turkey Table Favor

## WHAT YOU'LL NEED

1⅛-inch wood doll pin base

Wood balls: 1¾-inch diameter, 1¼-inch diameter

Wood teardrop cutouts: 11 large, 2 small

Acrylic paint: brown, yellow, red, orange

Paintbrushes

Low-temperature glue gun and glue sticks

Cardboard box

Acrylic spray sealer

Tracing paper

Pencil

Scissors

Felt: 1×2 inches orange, 1×2 inches red

2 wiggle eyes, 8mm each

Tweezers

**Adult help needed**

**1** Paint the wood pieces in the following colors: doll pin base, 1¾-inch ball, and 1¼-inch ball—brown; 4 large teardrops—yellow; 4 large teardrops—red; 3 large teardrops and 2 small teardrops—orange. Let dry, then apply a second coat of paint. Let dry completely.

**2** To make the turkey's body, glue the 1¾-inch ball to the doll pin base. For the head, glue the 1¼-inch wood ball to the front top of the body.

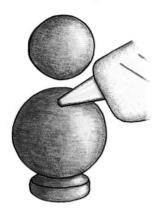

**3** Arrange the large teardrop pieces as shown in the illustration for the turkey's feathers. Overlap the edges of the teardrops and glue them together so they form a half circle of feathers. Glue the half circle of feathers to the body at the center and at each end of the half circle. To make the wings, glue a small teardrop to each side of the body. Put the turkey in a cardboard box in a well-ventilated area, and have an adult help you lightly spray it with acrylic sealer. Let dry.

**4** To make the beak, use the pattern below to trace and cut out 2 triangles from orange felt. Align the short sides of each triangle and glue them to the center front of the head. Use the pattern below to trace and cut out the wattle from red felt. Glue the top of the wattle to the head just below the beak. Glue the wiggle eyes to the turkey's head above the beak (you may want to use tweezers to help you with this).

## Patterns

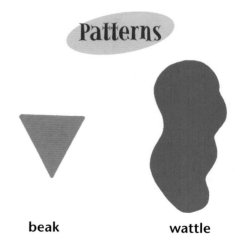

**beak**　　　**wattle**

# Halloween Mobile

## What You'll Need

Tracing paper

Pencil

Scissors

Craft foam: 5×5 inches yellow, 3×6 inches orange, 3×7 inches white, 5×5 inches black

Hole punch

Fine-point opaque paint markers: brown, black

Wiggle eyes: four 5mm, eighteen 12mm

Tweezers

Glue

58 inches black satin ribbon, ⅛ inch wide

Ruler

Black pom

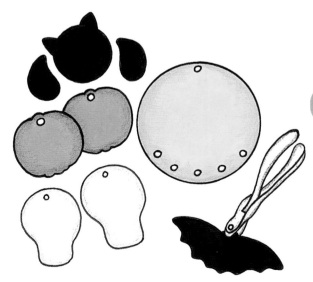

**1** Using the patterns on page 41, trace and cut out the following shapes from the craft foam: 1 yellow moon, 2 orange pumpkins (one of each outline), 2 white skulls, 1 black bat, 1 black cat head, and 2 black cat paws. Use the hole punch to make holes in the foam shapes as shown on the patterns.

**2** Draw lines on both sides of the pumpkins with the brown marker; use the black marker to make faces on both sides. Let dry. Draw faces on both sides of the skulls with the black marker; let dry. Use tweezers to glue two 5mm eyes on both sides of the bat. Glue two 12mm eyes on both sides of the pumpkins and skulls.

**3** Cut a 12-inch length of ribbon. Insert one end of the ribbon 1½ inches into the single hole at the top of the moon. Tie a double knot in the ribbon to securely attach it to the moon. Trim the short end of the ribbon close to the knot. Position and glue the cat head on the back upper side of the moon. Position and glue the cat paws on the front of the moon, with the right paw covering the ribbon hanger. Glue the black pom nose on the cat head so it slightly overlaps the edge of the moon, and glue two 12mm eyes to the cat head.

**4** Cut the remaining ribbon into the following lengths, and use double knots to tie one end of each length to a foam shape and the other end to a hole at the bottom of the moon: 6-inch length for 1 pumpkin, 9-inch length for 1 skull, 13-inch length for the bat; 11-inch length for 1 pumpkin, 7-inch length for 1 skull. Trim the ends of each length of ribbon close to the knots.

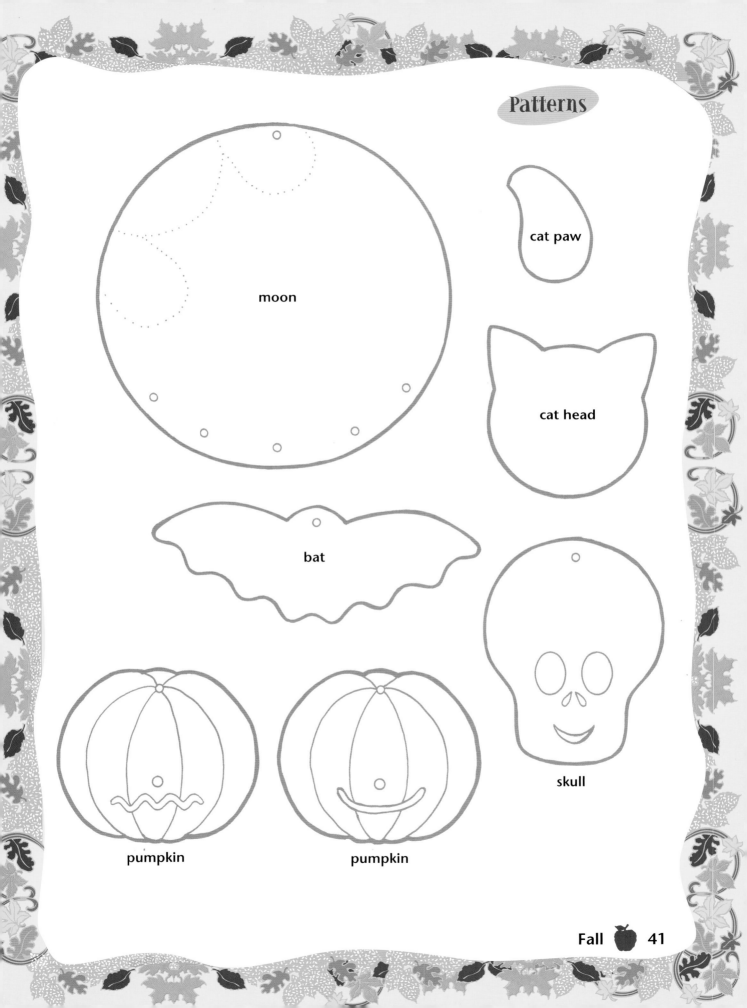

Patterns

moon

cat paw

cat head

bat

skull

pumpkin

pumpkin

# Back-to-School Beauties

Adult help needed

## Bulletin Board

**1** Measure the width of the inside of your locker door, and subtract 1 inch to determine the width of the bulletin board. The height for the board is 11 inches. Lay the foam core flat, then ask an adult to help you mark and cut out 2 pieces of foam core with the craft knife according to your measurements. Glue the pieces together.

**2** Position the scrapbook paper over the front of the foam core board (if needed, glue the side edges of 2 sheets of paper together to form 1 large sheet). Fold all the edges over to the back of the board and glue in place, smoothing out any bubbles or wrinkles as you glue.

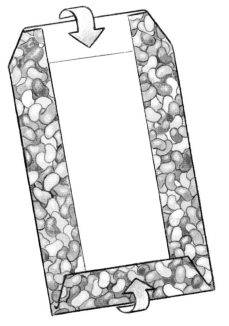

**3** Measure the width of the front of the bulletin board, and add 4 inches. Cut the ribbon to this measurement. Position the ribbon about ⅓ of the way down from the top of the bulletin board; glue the ribbon in place on the back of the board (leave the front unglued so you can slip notes behind the ribbon).

**4** To hang, apply one side of a hook-and-loop fastener to the back of the bulletin board. Attach the other side to the locker.

## Notebook Cover

**1** Position the scrapbook paper over the front of a notebook (if needed, glue the side edges of 2 sheets of paper together to form 1 large sheet). Cut a notch at the top and bottom of the paper where the notebook's spine falls. Then turn all the edges to the inside of the notebook and glue in place, smoothing out any bubbles and wrinkles.

**2** Measure the width of the front and back of the notebook, then add 16 inches. Cut the ribbon to this measurement. Position the ribbon around the center front and back of the notebook, and glue in place. When dry, tie the ribbons together at the book's opening edge.

### Try This!
You can make Back-to-School Beauties out of lots of things—textbooks, mini notepads, you name it! Just follow the basic techniques listed for the bulletin board and notebook cover.

# Harvest Bookmark

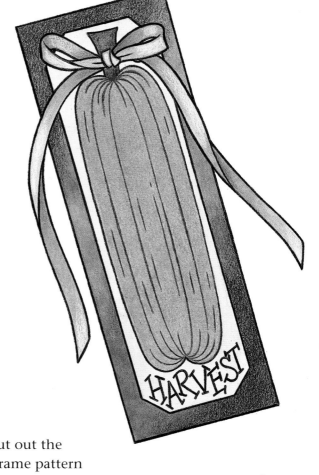

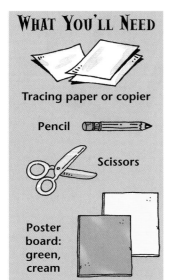

**1** Trace and cut out the bookmark frame pattern on page 46 from the green poster board. Repeat for the bookmark insert pattern (cream poster board) and the pumpkin (orange construction paper). If possible, use a copier to transfer the pumpkin pattern to orange construction paper so the detail lines will be visible. Otherwise, add the detail lines on the pumpkin with the black marker. Color in the stem with the brown marker.

**2** Glue the pieces together, stacking them on top of one another. Let dry 20 minutes. Write *HARVEST* below the pumpkin with black marker.

**3** Punch holes on both sides of the stem, insert the ribbon through the holes, and tie a bow at the base of the stem.

## Patterns

frame

insert

# Bat-Wing Bracelet

## WHAT YOU'LL NEED

Tracing paper

Pencil

Scissors

Black construction paper

Puffy paints

Glitter

Glue

Stapler and staples

Rubber band

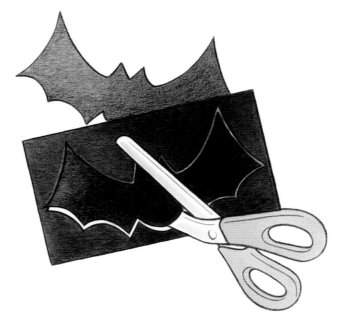

**1** Use the pattern on page 48 to trace and cut 2 or 3 bats out of black construction paper. Decorate the bats with puffy paints and glitter.

**2** When the bats are completely dry, stack 2 or 3 bats on top of each other. Staple the bats together in the center.

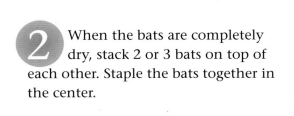

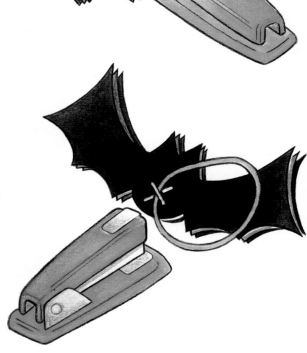

**3** Place a rubber band over the back of the staple, and staple the rubber band to the bats. Fan out the bat wings, and wear around your wrist as a spooky accessory!

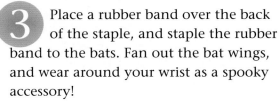

**Pattern**

# Christmas Window Decorations

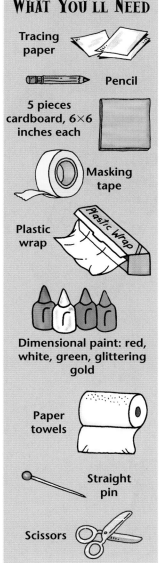

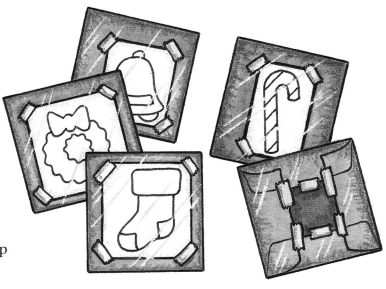

**1** Trace the patterns on page 51 onto individual pieces of paper, then tape each piece of paper to a piece of cardboard. Tightly cover each pattern with plastic wrap, and tape the edges of the plastic wrap to the back of the cardboard.

**2** Carefully paint the plastic wrap using the patterns as a guide (refer to the illustrations for color direction). Work with 1 color at a time, and let each color set for 10 minutes before you paint with the next color. Follow these tips for using dimensional paint: Outline the part of the pattern you're going to paint; lightly touch the tip of the bottle to the plastic wrap, carefully squeeze the bottle, and pull (don't push) the tip along the outline (the paint should be about ⅛ inch thick). Then paint inside the outlined area, working from left to right (or right to left if you're left-handed) and top to bottom. If you make a mistake, wipe the paint off with a paper towel. If the tip of the bottle clogs, use a straight pin to open the hole and then squeeze a bit of paint on a paper scrap to regain a smooth flow.

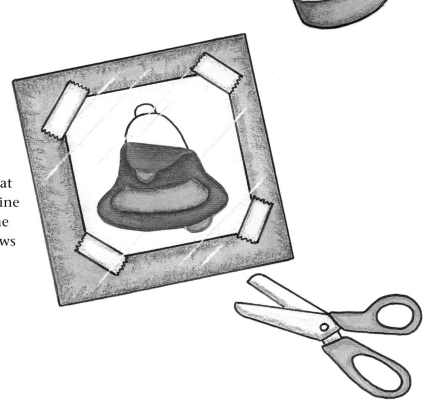

**3** Let the paint dry for 24 hours. Peel the decorations off the plastic wrap. Trim off any paint that has spread beyond the outline of the decorations. Hang the decorations on your windows for happy holiday cheer!

**Patterns**

# Heartbreaker

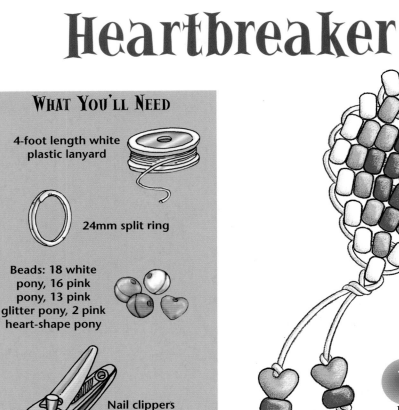

**1** Make a lark's head knot by folding the lanyard in half and slipping the looped end through the split ring. Pull the cut ends up through the loop; pull tight. Tie an overhand knot about ½ to 1 inch from the lark's head knot.

**2** String a white bead onto the left strand and slide it all the way up to the knot. Weave the right strand through the bead from right to left. To make the heart's upper arches, weave a "sidepath" by stringing beads 1–4 on the right strand. Leave a little space between the beads, and weave back through beads 1 and 2. Pull tightly as you weave back, allowing the beads to curve as shown. Repeat to make a sidepath with the left strand. Add a white bead on the end of each sidepath before you move on to the next row.

**3** String beads onto the left strand in the following order: 1 white, 2 pink, 1 pink glitter, 1 pink, 1 pink glitter, 2 pink, and 1 white. Weave the right strand through the same beads from right to left. Repeat this basic bead-weaving technique for the remaining rows, using the bead diagram for reference.

**4** Finish by tying both cord ends together in an overhand knot. To do this, twist both lanyard ends into a loop and then pull the free ends through the loop. Tie a second overhand knot on each cord about 1½ to 2 inches from the first knot. String a heart pony bead and a glitter bead on each cord, and finish each with another overhand knot. Trim the excess cord with the nail clippers, leaving ½-inch tails.

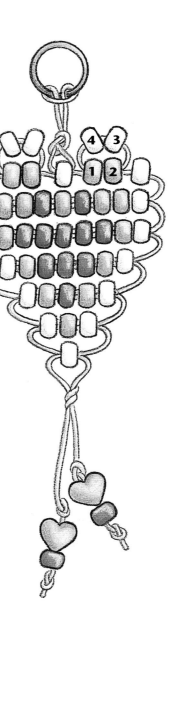

# Sensational Spiral Ornament

## What You'll Need

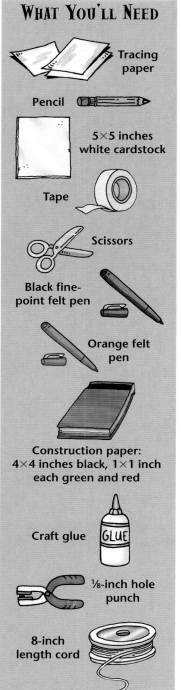

- Tracing paper
- Pencil
- 5×5 inches white cardstock
- Tape
- Scissors
- Black fine-point felt pen
- Orange felt pen
- Construction paper: 4×4 inches black, 1×1 inch each green and red
- Craft glue
- 1/8-inch hole punch
- 8-inch length cord

**1** Trace or photocopy the patterns on page 55. Tape the spiral pattern to the cardstock, and cut along the lines of the pattern. Remove the pattern.

**2** Draw the eyes, nose, and mouth on the head (the center of the spiral) using the black felt pen. Color the nose orange. Fold the head upward.

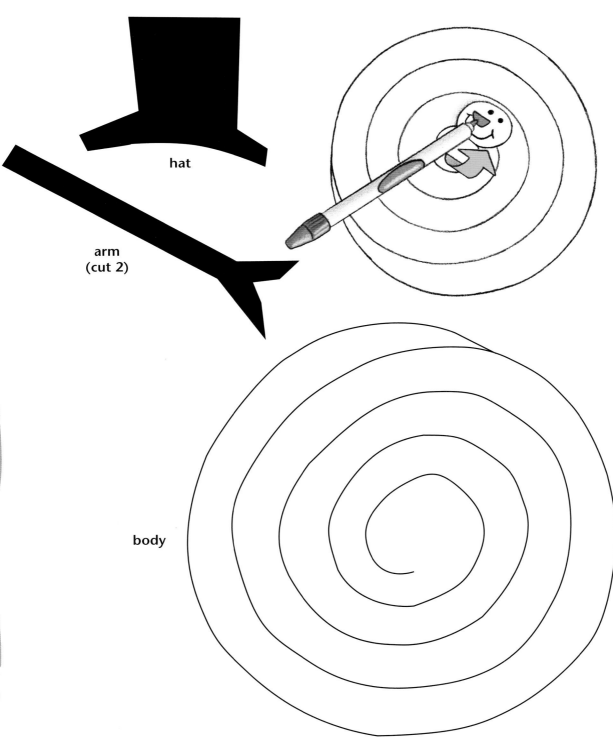

**hat**

**arm (cut 2)**

**body**

**3** Cut out the patterns for the arm and the hat. Trace around the arm pattern twice on the black paper and cut out. Fold the remaining piece of black paper in half, and place the top edge of the hat pattern along the fold. Trace around the pattern, and cut it out (don't cut the fold). Apply glue to the inside of the hat, and slip it over the snowman's head. Press the hat pieces together, sandwiching the top of the head between. Glue an arm to each side of the first spiral below the head.

**4** From the green paper, cut out 2 holly leaves. Use the hole punch to make a red berry from the red paper. Glue the holly leaves and the berry to the hat.

**5** Punch a hole in the top of the hat. Fold the cord in half and tie the ends of the cord together. Push the cord loop through the hole, and thread the tied ends of the cord through the loop of the cord. Hang your spiral friend on a Christmas tree or wherever you like!

## What You'll Need

- **Tracing paper**
- **Pencil**
- **Scissors**
- **Pennant felt:** 11×13 inches gold, 17×20 inches blue, 3½×7 inches white
- **18-inch wood dowel,** ½ inch diameter
- **2 wood doll pin bases,** 1⅛ inches each
- **2 wood head beads,** 1¼ inches each
- **Cardboard box**
- **Gold spray paint**
- **Ruler**
- **Low-temperature glue gun and glue sticks**
- **19-inch length gold fringe,** 4 inches wide
- **Masking tape**
- **28-inch length gold metallic cord**

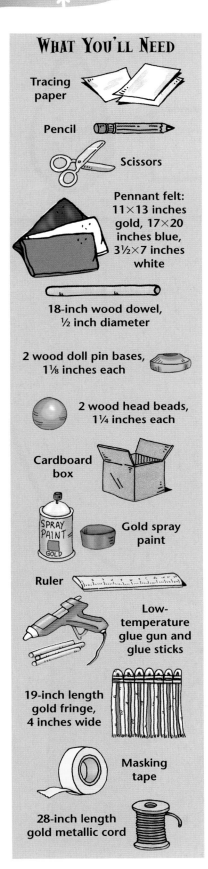

**1** Using the pattern on page 58, trace and cut out the menorah from the gold felt. Working with an adult in a well-ventilated area, place the menorah, the dowel, the 2 doll pin bases, and the 2 head beads in the cardboard box. Spray all with 2 coats of gold spray paint. Let dry.

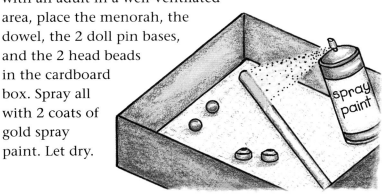

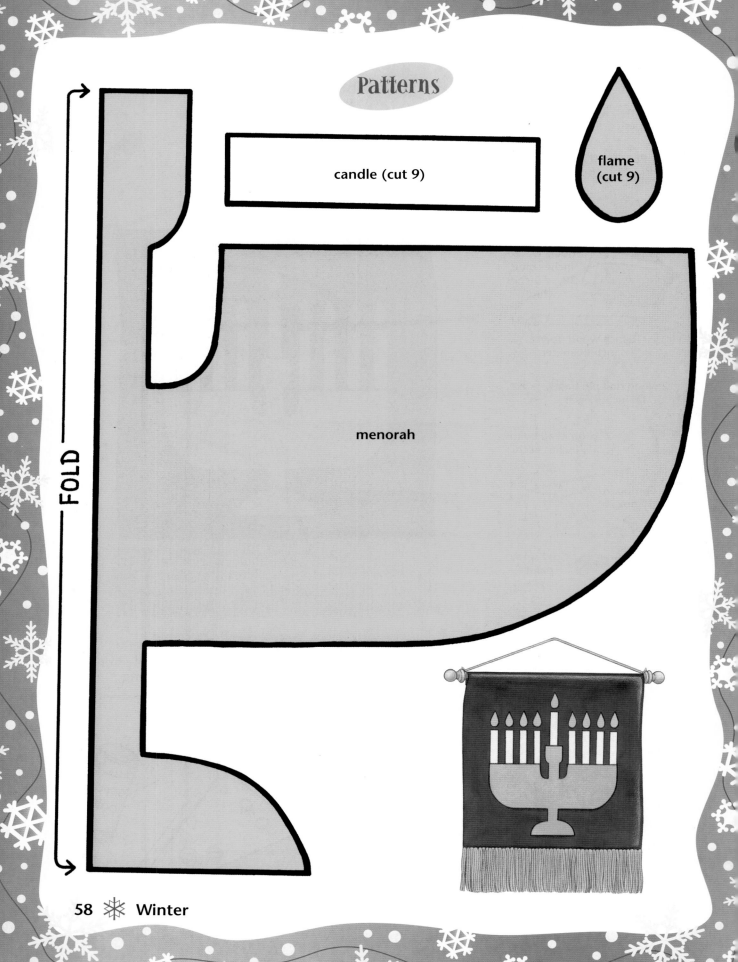

# Patterns

candle (cut 9)

flame (cut 9)

FOLD

menorah

**2** To make a hem in the 17-inch side of the blue felt, fold over 2 inches of the felt and crease it. Unfold, then apply a line of glue ¼ inch from the edge and refold the felt. Hold it in place until the glue dries. Be sure to leave enough room between the crease and the glue line to insert the dowel.

**4** Glue the fringe to the bottom of the banner so 1 inch of fringe sticks out from each side. Fold and glue the 1-inch sections of fringe to the back of the banner. Position the menorah and candles as shown in the illustration, then glue them to the banner. For each day of Hanukkah, roll a piece of masking tape into a loop with the sticky side out, put on the back of a flame, and add to the banner.

**3** Using the patterns on page 58, trace and cut out 9 candles from the white pennant felt and 9 flames from the gold felt.

**5** Slide the dowel through the hem at the top of the banner. Glue a head bead to a doll pin base, then glue them to one end of the dowel. Repeat on the other end of the dowel. To make a hanger, tie the ends of the cord to the ends of the dowel.

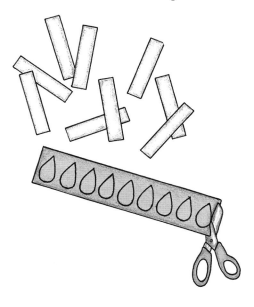

# My Kwanzaa Family

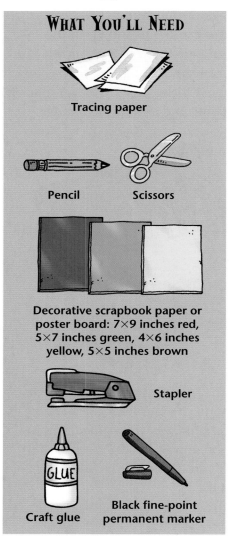
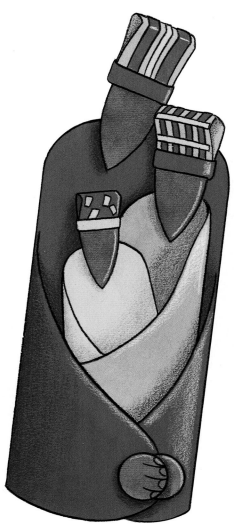

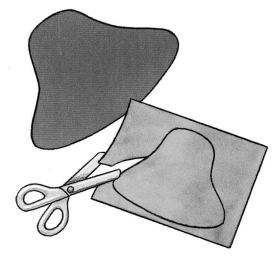

1. Trace and cut out the father's body pattern from page 61 on red poster board or scrapbook paper. Repeat for the mother's body pattern using green paper and the child's body pattern using yellow paper. Trace and cut out 2 head patterns for the mother and father, 1 child's head, and 2 father's hands from brown paper. Trace and cut out 2 hat patterns for the mother and father using green paper and 1 child's hat pattern from red paper. Set aside.

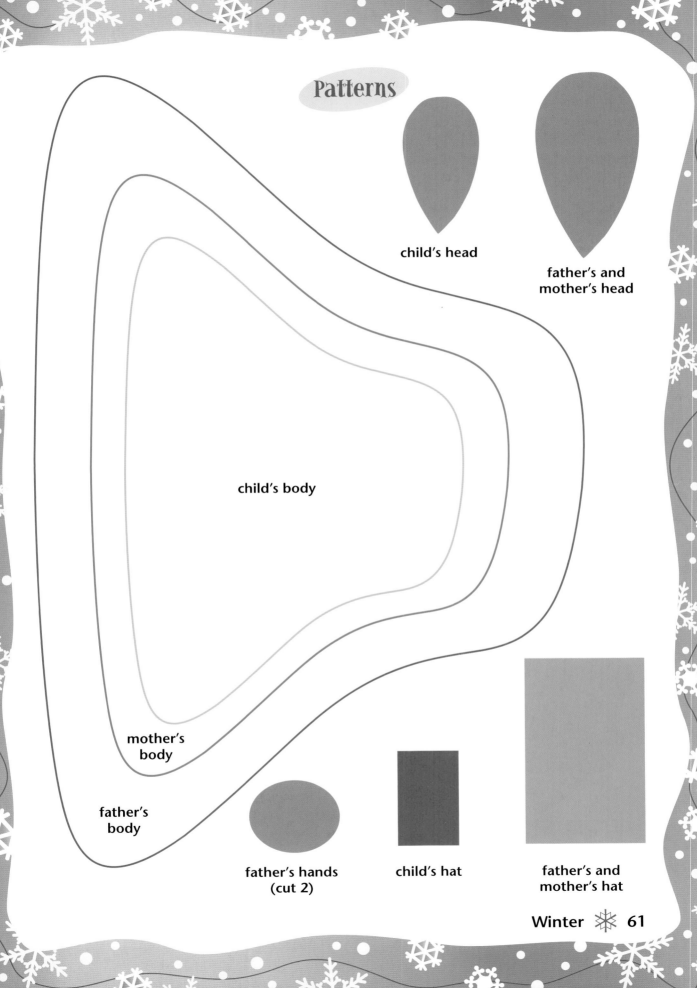

**Patterns**

child's head

father's and
mother's head

child's body

mother's
body

father's
body

father's hands
(cut 2)

child's hat

father's and
mother's hat

**2** Bring the "arm" parts of the father's "body" together, overlapping the arms in front and stapling them together. Repeat with mother and child cutouts. Glue heads onto the bodies of the mother, father, and child.

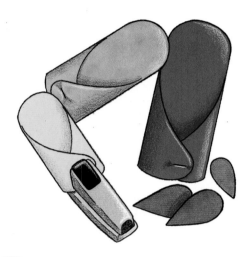

**3** Decorate the hats with leftover paper or poster board scraps. Let dry. Fold the father's hat in half, bringing the short ends together, and staple or glue the hat to the father's head. Glue a strip of paper around the bottom of the hat to cover the staple and look like a hatband. Repeat for the mother's hat and the child's hat.

**4** Insert the bodies one inside the other, turning them so the child is cradled at the center of the family. Draw the fingers on the father's hands with the black marker, then glue them to the front.

### Did You Know?

Kwanzaa means "the first" or "the first fruits of the harvest" in Kiswahili. (Kiswahili is an East African language.) Dr. Maulana Karenga began the holiday in 1966 to celebrate the rich cultural roots of African-American people.